THE
Archive Photographs
SERIES

UPPER RHONDDA
TREORCHY AND TREHERBERT

A Rhondda family from the late Victorian period sitting proudly in the photographer's studio, *c*. 1889. Mr David W. Joseph and his wife Jennet of No 142 Dumfries Street, Treherbert are pictured with their five children: Jennet, Elizabeth and Thomas (back row), Mary and David (sitting).

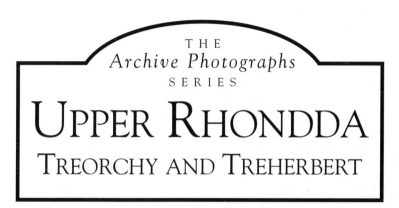

THE
Archive Photographs
SERIES

UPPER RHONDDA
TREORCHY AND TREHERBERT

Compiled by
Emrys Jenkins and Roy Green from their own collections
and those of many other Rhondda people.

CHALFORD

First published 1997
Copyright © Emrys Jenkins and Roy Green, 1997

The Chalford Publishing Company
St Mary's Mill, Chalford,
Stroud, Gloucestershire, GL6 8NX

ISBN 0 7524 1016 4

Typesetting and origination by
The Chalford Publishing Company
Printed in Great Britain by
Bailey Print, Dursley, Gloucestershire

This book is dedicated to our grandchildren: Leanne Coombs; Thomas, Timothy, Alex, Daniel and Ben Jenkins; Zoe and Leon Elston; Matthew, Jessica, Sarah, Shaun and Alex Green, and also to the memory of Jack Hart and Cyril Lewis.

From left to right: Roy Green, Jack Hart, Cyril Lewis, Emrys Jenkins.

Contents

Bryn Lisle (left, with lamp) overman at Glenrhondda Colliery (known as the 'Hook and Eye'), Blaencwm. He is pictured in 1963 with D.S. Evans the colliery manager.

Introduction

By former County Councillor Bryn Lisle

This is the third in a series of books containing a compilation of photographs portraying the past history of the Rhondda. Emrys Jenkins, Roy Green and Simon Eckley have painted a broad canvas of life in the Rhondda using the images captured by the camera lens rather than an artist's brush and palette.

It is a book that will evoke nostalgia in the present generation and will be a source of education for the younger ones. For those of the older generation it will bring back memories of industry and life in what was once the most famous coal-producing valley in the world. The book will be of particular interest to those who have left our valley to make new lives in lands far overseas, and in other areas of Britain, but who still retain a love for their homeland.

The changing face of the valley, as we know it now, is vividly brought to life by these pictures of days long gone. Most of the pictures remind us of happy times, euphemistically called the 'good old days' by some people. However, we must never forget that they were not all good days. There is nothing good in our past history when we hear of children working in the coal mines. Conditions were not much better in the 1930s when, from my own experience, one went down the pit at 14 years of age and worked six days for a wage of 12s 4d and we must never forget the legacy of broken bodies which still suffer the effects of coal mining in Rhondda.

In consecutive years from 1990 to 1993, and in 1995, exhibitions of photographs and old documents were held in Treherbert's OAP Hall, entitled 'Down Memory Lane'. These exhibitions aroused a tremendous response, and much interest from the public, not only locally but from places far away – thanks to publicity on the radio.

Unfortunately, the human mind can only retain memories for a

12-year-old Hospital Schools Queen Olwen Demaid is crowned by out-going Queen, Irene Parsons, on the steps of Treherbert Hospital, 1930.

comparatively short time and therefore this book is of paramount importance as we will now be able to take a stroll 'down memory lane' each time we look through it. One will never fail to be impressed by the character of Rhondda people who have held on to a sense of humour in the face of great adversity.

I give the authors my very best wishes for the success of this excellent book.

One
Cwmparc

T. Tortello, ice-cream vendor in Cwmparc, c. 1920.

Staff at Park School, *c.* 1910.

Staff at Park School, *c.* 1913.

The Morgan family, Cwmparc, *c.* 1905.
From left to right, back row: Thomas,
William, John, Evan. Middle row: Mary
Jane, Martha, Rebecca, Margaret, Alice.
Front row: Ben, Mr John Morgan, Emlyn,
Mrs Ann Morgan, Kathy. John Morgan
was preceptor of Salem Chapel, Cwmparc.
The Morgans were a well-known musical
family and were locally referred to as the
'Bassos', because of their singing abilities.

Cwmparc Temperance group, *c.* 1895.

Dare Colliery, Cwmparc, *c*. 1910. This colliery closed in 1964.

Park Colliery, Cwmparc, showing the wooden headgear of No 1 pit, *c*. 1905. The colliery closed
in 1967.

End of the 'stay-in' strike at the Dare Colliery, October 1935.

The 'stay-in' comrades, Dare Colliery, October 1935. From left to right, back row: H. Heard, T. Payne, M. Jones, -?-, J. Phillips, -?-, E. Edwards, W. Lewis, W. Jones, A. Jones, F. Young. Middle row: J. Williams, F. Roberts, R. Vincent, ? Eddy, Cllr I.R. Thomas, -?-, D. Chislett, T. Smith. Front row: -?-, W. May (Miners' Agent), V. Evans, I. Edwards.

Surface craftsman and workmen at Park Colliery. Back row: -?-, Alan Smith, -?-. Third row: -?-, Tom Waite, Hubert Davies. Second row: David James, Idris Griffiths. Front row: Billy Williams, -?-.

Park and Dare Lodge Committee, 1952. From left to right, back row: George Baker, J. Jeremiah, George Everleigh, -?-, Will Scott, Glyn Wilkins, Will Coles, Stan Millard, W.H. Williams, C. Tidy. Middle row: I. Thomas, G. Rees, Alcwyn Meredith, Tom Evans, E. Lloyd, Ken Davies, Ray Jenkins. Front row: I. Winter, G. Meredith, Austin Pearce, Dai 'Bogo' Thomas, Gordon 'Dusty' Lewis.

Dare Colliery concert party – The Dareites, 1950. From left to right: Billy Davies, Wyndham King, Ieuan Watkins, Hedley Curtis, Roy Williams, Cliff Giles, Mansel Candy, George Collins, Reg Edwards, Mrs Sheridan (sitting), Aneurin Sheridan, Cyril Phillips, Ned Knapgate, Emrys Lloyd, Billy Griffiths, Iori Williams. The Dareites were active from 1949 to 1952, performing in local clubs and outside the Rhondda to raise money for charity. They were disbanded in 1952 after the tragic loss of musical director Ieuan Watkins, who died following a motor-cycle accident.

The Dareites Comic Band, 1950. From left to right: Billy Griffiths, Billy Davies, Reg Edwards, Cliff Giles, Aneurin Sheridan, Ned Knapgate, Ieuan Watkins, George Collins.

Lower end of Cwmparc, *c*. 1908.

Standard 1B at Park Infant School, 1931.

Standard 5B at Cwmparc Boys' School, 1931. Amongst those pictured: Doug Watkins, John Owen, Norman Townsend, Ray Flagons, David Thomas, Don Davies, Elwyn Morris, Bill Sibley, Denver Mundy, Alwyn Jones, Ken Higgon, Bernard Chappell, Bill Spiller, Trefor Jones (aka 'Wireless Pole', teacher, on left), Eddie George, H.C. Curtis, Eddie Mardy, Les Davies, Ron Morris, Ken Jones, Steve Camale, George Owen, Jack Jeremiah, Billy Chopin, Dai Morgan, Moelwyn Jones, Dai Rees (headmaster, on right).

Soar Welsh Congregational Chapel, Cwmparc, *c.* 1921.

Park Road, Cwmparc, *c.* 1910. On the right at No 214 is Evan Evans, newsagent's and further down the road on the left is Park Chapel.

A prize-winning horse and trap belonging to Ebenezer Brown, baker at No 263 Park Road, Cwmparc, *c.* 1920.

Two Cwmparc lads dressed up for carnival time, *c*. 1926.

Cwmparc Drum & Fife Band, early this century. Formed in 1893, it was later to change its name to the Cwmparc Silver Band.

Park & Dare Band, *c.* 1928. Featured in the photograph are Ieuan Humphries, Will Williams, Jack Smith, Lewis Brown, Stan Bebb, Harry Thomas, Emlyn Morgan, Trevor Morgan and Griff Higgon.

Class 1 at Park Junior Mixed School in costume as part of Festival of Britain celebrations, 1951.

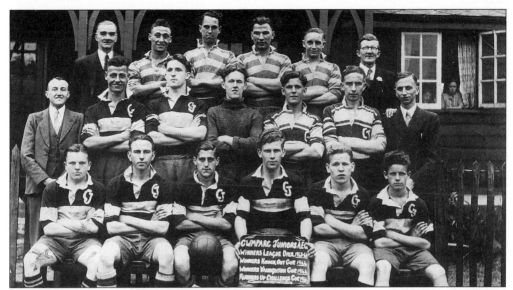

Cwmparc Juniors AFC, 1943-44. Due to the shortages of the war the team played in different style shirts as they could not get a full set. The captain and vice-captain have wider hoops on their shirts. The reserves are at the back. From left to right, back row: Ned Edwards, Les Davies, Ronnie Jones, Dai Watkins, Dai Fox, Reg Edwards. Middle row: George Williams, Donald Davies, John Jones, Doug Pearce, Tom Thomas, Glan Powell, Jack Hughes. Front row: John Lawry, Ron Dowling, Mansel Samuel, Maurice Jenkins, Cliff 'Bubbles' Evans, Fred 'Curly' Thomas.

Cwmparc Juniors football team a few years later, c. 1947. From left to right, back row: Tom Davies ('Noisy'), Reg Edwards, George Williams, John Lawry, Jack Jones ('Peat'). Middle row: Cyril Jenkins, Morris Jenkins, Jack Knapgate, Emo Lewis, Elwyn Jenkins, Freddie Thomas ('Curly'). Front row: Ron Jones, Freddie Edwards, Tommy Thomas, Billy Glass, Mansel Samuel.

Coronation party outside the Dare Hotel in Park Road, 1953. From left to right, front row: Mrs Higgs, Mrs Bebb, Mr Bebb, Betty Shepherd, Nancy Jones, -?-, -?-, Mary Higgs, Mrs Lewis ('Travellers'). Back row: Mrs Watkins (far left); behind Mr Bebb is Tom Davies ('Noisy'); behind the men in the Dai caps is Glyn Morgan.

Dare Colliery canteen staff together with fitters and saddlers, c. 1947. They are pictured on the flat roof of the baths. From left to right: Cliff Bound, Derrick Williams, Phyllis Watkins, David Samuel, Mrs Evans, Katy Vaughan, George Clarke, Cliff Giles.

Two
Treorchy

Cardiff Arms Square, *c.* 1915, showing Treorchy Conservative Club on the left.

Abergorki Colliery, *c*. 1900. The pit shaft here was sunk in 18`65 by George Insole.

Upper Treorchy, *c*. 1938. Tylacoch Place is front left; the Salvation Army Hall (now a tyre centre) is across the railway and river; Ramah Chapel can be seen at the edge of the huge tip while Abergorki Colliery is in the background behind it.

Bute Street, Treorchy, looking up the valley, *c*. 1900.

Further up Bute Street, *c*. 1902.

Station Road, *c.* 1900.

Looking back down Station Road to the junction with Bute Street/High Street, *c.* 1915.

Treorky Boot Repairing Staff, 1926.

Joseph Jones, boot repairer and maker, No 155 Bute Street, Treorchy, c. 1920.

Left: Mrs Balestrazzi with Mrs Rogers (centre) who kept a butcher's shop near the present Boots store and Phyllis Richards (right) who worked in the cafe, *c*. 1932. *Right*: the same cafe under its new name. Owner Dom Balestrazzi is pictured with daughters Gina and Rita, *c*. 1935.

Bute Street, *c*. 1920.

High Street, Treorchy. 415.

High Street, Treorchy, with workmen busy with picks outside the Prince of Wales public house prior to the National Eisteddfod in 1928. The small gardens in front of the houses were all removed in one day to widen the road. Gordon Stores can be clearly seen on the right.

High Street, Treorchy, *c.* 1912.

Ystradfechan House, *c*. 1910. Mr W. Jenkins, colliery agent-manager, was the first tenant of this company house. He started the first school in Cwmparc which was housed in a loft over the colliery stables and had one class for pupils aged between eight and eighteen. Jenkins was succeeded at Ystradfechan House by Mr Edwards, (colliery agent), Mr W.P. Thomas and finally Levi Phillips. The house was demolished and there is now a home for senior citizens on the site.

Dr Fergus Armstrong with Pentwyn Hospital staff, *c*. 1928.

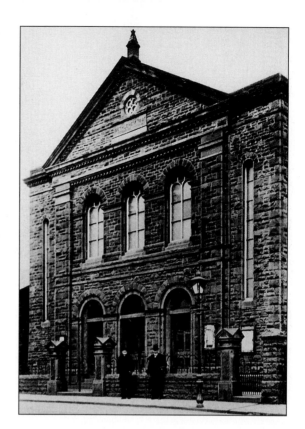

Bethlehem Chapel, High Street, Treorchy, *c*. 1909. Standing outside are Parch. T. Davies (minister) and Mr D. Peters (leader and elder).

Treorchy Zulus South Wales Tableau Champions, possibly pictured in Cardiff, 1926. During the Miners' Strike of 1926 unemployed men throughout South Wales filled the long summer with self-made entertainment.

Bardic ceremony at the National Eisteddfod of Wales held at Treorchy, 9 August 1928.

M. Long, Treorchy fishmonger, out on his rounds, *c*. 1928. His shop was next-door to Noddfa Chapel.

The Parc and Dare Hall, Treorchy was opened in 1903 as a workmen's institute and library.

The Parc and Dare Cinema can clearly be seen beginning to tower over the surrounding Treorchy streets in this picture taken during its construction (1912-13).

Treorchy Co-operative Stores, Bute Street, 1920s.

Mr Bracey, a shoe repairer, had emigrated to America and when he returned to the Rhondda he brought back the latest advertising techniques having the first shop in the Treorchy area with an illuminated sign.

Children's playground, Treorchy, *c.* 1939.

The EMI factory, *c.* 1952. The four white roofs were replacements after the fire in 1950 which destroyed three of the bays. The T.C. Jones factory is on the left.

Treorchy Rugby Football Club, pictured at the opening of new grounds, 26 January 1924. From left to right, back row: C. Evans, G. Edwards, S. Jones, D. Thomas, R. Collins, George Griffiths, Con. Griffiths, Isaac Hinton, H. Millward. Second row: H. Skym, D.W. Jones (Trainer), E. Skym, R. Hughes, Jack Harris, A. Culverhouse, Ivor Rowlands, Tom Davies, E. Enoch, W.D. James, Wyndham Lewis. Front row: T.G. Hopkins (Hon. Secretary), A. John, George Collins (Vice-Captain), E. Boynes, D. Cennamo (Vice-President), Daley James (Captain), Stan Jones, Jack John, G.H. Pritchard (Hon. Treasurer). Seated: J. Bryn Jones, Ken James, D.R. Morgan.

Pentre Secondary School RFC, 1938-39 season. A number of Treorchy lads are among those pictured. From left to right, standing: Eddy Thomas, -?-, -?-, -?-, -?-, Gwyn Martin, Billy Mathias, -?-, -?-. Seated: Mr Martin, -?-, -?-, -?-, Elfed Owen, Billy Cleaver, Mr Richards (headmaster). Cross-legged: -?-, -?-, -?-, Teifryn Parry.

The successful Treorchy Boys' Club basketball team of the late 1940s. They were Welsh Association of Boys' Clubs (WABC) junior champions in the 1946-47 season and WABC senior champions in 1947-48. From left to right, back row: Roy Evans, Derek Davies, Howard Jones, John Francis, David Hughes. Front row: Albert H. Nicholas (Trainer and Coach), David James, Gwyn Davies (Captain), Desmond Goodridge, Stanley T. Hughes (Supervisor and Organiser).

Treorchy Comprehensive School rugby team, 1969-70 season.

Standard 2A at Treorchy Junior School, 1931. This year – like 1913 – saw the visit of George Holdsworth & Son, 'scholastic photo specialists' of Hartlepool to schools throughout the Rhondda. Although business was evidently the sole reason for this work, today we can be grateful that such a comprehensive record of a generation of Rhondda children has been left for posterity.

Class 4G at Treorchy Infant School, 1931.

Sergeant Major Eddie Hughes heads his platoon of Home Guards, outside Station Road Chapel, Treorchy, *c.* 1941.

Treorchy post office staff, 1945. From left to right, back row: M. Jones, T. Morgan, E.W. Davies, J.L. Jones, D.J. Mills, J.R. Evans, D. Hughes, D. Wiltshire. Second row: P. Lewis, C. Curtis, E.J. Evans, A. Griffiths, J. Thomas, J.M. Lloyd, T.H. Goodridge, R.M. Thomas, E.J. Davies, G. Morgan. Front row: S. Amos, D. Williams, V.R. Weeks, E.H.J. Richards, P.A. James, W.E. Rumsey (Postmaster), E.J. Davies, M. Jones, A. Evans, A. Thomas, G. Davies.

Royal Welsh Male Choir, Treorchy, 1924. From left to right, back row: David Thomas, George Jones, Gomer Williams, John Evans, Steve James (soloist), Ivor Foster (soloist), James Jaynes, David J. Thomas. Second row: William Morgan, William Phillips, Isaac Rees, David Powell, Evan Davies, John Jones. Front row: Thomas Thomas (Treasurer), David Davies (Secretary and soloist), Miss May John (soprano soloist), Gwilym T. Jones (conductor), Rd. Davies (accompanist), John J. Thomas (Chairman), Idris Thomas, Gomer Williams (soloist).

Children dressed as Ancient Britons and Romans during the Pageant of the Rhondda, c. 1949. Three schools were involved: Treorchy, Treherbert and Bronllwyn. Among those pictured: Dewi Jones, Emrys Lewis, Bobby Llewellyn, David Pickens, Sylvia John, Mair Harris, Derek Watkins, Des Richards, John Loney, Alwyn Jones.

Treorchy Male Choir pictured on the move in London *c.* 1950 when they sung at the National Coal Board Boxing Tournament Finals.

Working committee of the Urdd National Eisteddfod which was held at Treorchy in 1947. *Pwyllgor gwaith, Eisteddfod Genedlaethol yr Urdd, Treorci, 1947.*

The cup won by the Treorchy Male Choir at the National Eisteddfod, Caernarfon, 1959.

Treorchy Secondary School Youth Band at the *Daily Herald* National Brass Band Finals, Fourth Section, Hammersmith Town Hall, 24 October 1959. From left to right, back row: D. Skym, G. Fitzpatrick, P. Morgan, T. Herbert, A. Davies, C. Jeremiah, K. Lewis. Middle row: W. Glass, G. Thomas, W. Hughes, M. Owen, H. Evans, C. Lindsey, P. Griffiths, M. Pugh, A. Morgan, L. Gibbs, R. Hearn. Front row: M. Pickin, M. Folwer, J. Pugh, R. Thomas, Mr I. Morgan, B. Price, D. Jones, R. Jones. This youth band proved a fine nursery of talent which fed into the senior bands of the area.

Three
Ynyswen and Penyrenglyn

The Royal Exchange Hotel, *c*. 1900, later Jimmy Oliver's shop.

Children and adults in their Sunday best at what may have been a Whitsun chapel gathering in Ynysfelin Field, *c.* 1914. The white buildings next to the tree in the centre of the picture are River Row, while up the hill, top left of picture, the newly-completed terraces of Herbert Street and Ynysfeio Avenue can be clearly seen. The inscription on the building (centre left) reads 'Geo. Kirkhouse Carpenter and Builder'.

Amidst a huge crowd that had assembled to witness the occasion, Councillor Rhys Morgan Rees unveils a plaque at the official opening of Ynysfeio railway bridge, May 1927.

Blacksmith shop at Ynysfeio Colliery, *c.* 1920.

No 1 rescue team at Ynysfeio Colliery, *c.* 1920. From left to right, back row: M. Thorne, Bert Griffiths, Glyn Grant, George Maurice (Captain). Front row: Syd Vest, John Jenkins, William Williams.

Ynyswen Road, 1920s.

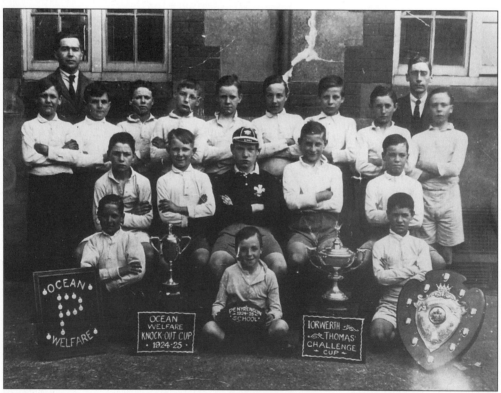

The successful 1924-25 Penyrenglyn School rugby team, winners of the Ocean Welfare Knock-out Cup and the Iorwerth Thomas Challenge Cup. The schoolboy international is Tommy Jayne.

Staff of the Carmel Chapel soup kitchen which was set up to alleviate the suffering during the 1926 Miners' Strike. From left to right, back row: Sam Williams, Joe Todd, Mr Henry, -?-, Mr Todd-Jones, Mr Howard, Mr Evans, -?-. Second row: Mel Grant, Mrs Grant, Alice Jenkins, Mrs Brazel, Mrs Williams, Mrs Todd-Jones, Mrs Parry. Front row: Henry Goodfellow, -?-, -?-, Owen Hughes, Mr Thomas (holding Gwyn Thomas), Glyn Grant.

Members of Penuel Chapel Sunday school dressed for a performance of *Sarah the Captive Maid*, 27 January 1938.

Class 1A at Penyrenglyn Infants' School, 1913.

Penyrenglyn Infants' School, c. 1927. The boy sitting on the floor near the basket is Merlyn Todd-Jones.

Penyrenglyn Schools RFC posing proudly with cups and shield at the end of the 1927-28 season.

Ynyswen School, c. 1910. These buildings were later demolished due to subsidence and Ynyswen Welfare Hall (known locally as 'The Coffin') now occupies the site.

Penyrenglyn School rugby team, 1919-20 season. From left to right, back row: Mr E. Player, Mr M. Protheroe, Mr P. Davies, Mr B. Haddock, Mr W. Lewis. Third row: T. Bowen, R. Hitchings, H.J. Cullen, T. Protheroe, E. Hopkin, W. Hughes, W. Evans. Second row: T. Morgan, G. Parry, Mr W.J. Gruar, Mr J. Phillips, Mr B. Nicholas, G. Addis, W. Beach. Front row: W. Edwards, A. Thomas, E. Davies, F. Smith (Captain), D. Morgan, D. Evans, M. Todd-Jones.

Class A at Penyrenglyn Infant School, 1931.

Staff at Ynyswen Junior School, 1929.

Group 7 at Ynyswen Junior School, 1931.

Group 2 at Ynyswen Junior School, 1931. The teacher is Miss Thomas.

Baglan Quoit Club, winners of the Rhondda League Challenge Cup, 1935. From left to right, back row: I. Barnes, C. Barnes, S. Saunders, J. Williams, G. Jones, J. Jones, J. Barnes. Front row: S. Evans (kneeling), S. Hart, W. Williams, W. Hart, E. Nation, J. Williams, J. Penhale (kneeling). D. Williams holds the cup.

Keep-fit class at the National schoolrooms, Mount Libanus Street, c. 1936. From left to right, back row: J. Pratt, Spencer Williams, Gil Foley, Merlin Todd Jones, Haydn Bundock, Gwyn Williams, -?-, Tom Bryant, Sam Duncan, Will Hughes, Will Bundock. Middle row: ? Griffiths, Nana Preece, Lil Wootton, John Hughes, Jack Greenhill, Marion Woolfe, Haydn Harris, ? Evans, Sid Fews, Alan Beauchamp, Nancy Grant. Front row: Benny Pratt, Glennie Walters, ? Soley, Nancy Evans, Roy Duncan, Mair Protheroe, -?-, Nancy Davies.

Staff at the new Polikoff Factory, c. 1939. From left to right, back row: Frank Godfrey, -?-, Johnny Westacott, -?-, Mr Harman, Arthur Spiller, Bill Jones. Second row: Mr Winkle, -?-, -?-, Miss Surridge, Miss Draper, Nellie White, -?-, -?- Miss Kimble, Miss Webster, -?-, Lillian Griffiths. Front row: -?-, Tilly John, -?-, Nana Millward, Alec Goldstein, Doris Billingham, Edith Burrows, Mrs Mago, -?-, Mair Morgan.

The Polikoff Factory building, *c.* 1950.

Polikoff's office staff, 1947. From left to right, back row: Tegwen Evans, Gwenda Morgan, Margaret Davies, Valerie Jarman. Front row: Shirley Jones, Peggy Harvey, Mair Jones, Valmai Casam.

The Ynyswen Ladies (Factory) Choir, May 1950. From left to right, back row: Tegwen ?, Nana Millward, Peggy Jones, Nancy Fletcher, -?-, Audrey Jones, Betty Chown, Iris Jones, Nancy Watkins. Third row: Nancy Oats, Nellie Thomas, -?-, Muriel Aubrey, -?-, -?-, -?-, -?-, Margaret Moon, Tegwen Williams, Thelma Moon. Second row: Mair Morgan, Tilly John, Betty Haytor, Joan Golding, -?-, Mrs Jones, Lorraine Colwill, Doris Morgan, -?-, Gladys Davies, -?-, Lizzie Bowen. Front row: Mr Thomas, Mrs Farmer, Betty Baxter, Olwen Edwards (conductor), Mr Luck, G. Lewis (pianist), -?-, Gerty Nicholas, Doris Billingham, Mr Livings (choir secretary).

These men all worked in the press-room at Polikoff's. The occasion is the 1958 Christmas dinner-dance. From left to right, back: Jimmy Pitt, Roy Jarman, Idwal Brace. Second 'row': Elwyn Jones, Elwyn Woolson, John Thomas, -?-, Gwyn Bebb, Ivor Bassett (glasses), Ivor Walters, Glyn Rees, -?-, Bernard Shanklyn, Barbara Jones. Front row: -?-, John Morgan, Keith Rowe, Graham Phillips, Ron Exell, John Jones.

Corbett Street women's football team, 1969.

Left: Gwilym Tanner of Herbert Street, Penyrenglyn, dressed up to kick off the Treherbert Town Women's Football match held during the Investiture celebrations, July 1969. *Right*: Ivor Mace pictured at National Kelsae Onion Festival at Harrogate in 1987 where he broke the world record for the heaviest Kelsae – an achievement that secured him a place in the *Guiness Book of Records*. The mammoth onion weighed in at 8lb 13.5oz.

Four
Treherbert

Group of men outside Rabaiotti Bros. refreshment rooms, No 171 Bute Street, Treherbert, *c.* 1920.

Standing in the doorway of his ironmonger's shop is D. Davies, father of the well-known Handel and Garnet Davies who continued their undertaking business until the late 1970s. Items which can be seen in front of the shop include shovels, hatchets, sledgehammers and the 'curling boxes' which were used to fill coal in the old 'stall and heading' system of work.

Alan Gitsham, Bute Street saddler, *c.* 1909.

Bute Street, Treherbert, *c.* 1912.

Bute Street, Treherbert, *c.* 1925. The Gaiety Cinema can be seen on the left. This was demolished in 1970 and the site is now occupied by a Spar supermarket.

Station Street, Treherbert, *c*. 1912, with the Opera House dominating the right of picture.

Singers in costume for a performance of *Hywel a Blodwen* at the Opera House in Treherbert, *c*. 1910. Sitting is soprano Miriam Parfitt (*née* Davies) of Blaenrhondda and standing is tenor Idris Daniels of Swansea. Composed by Joseph Parry, *Hywel a Blodwen* was the first Welsh-language Grand opera.

Treherbert Drum & Fife Band, 1912. The conductor was Mr G. Edwards.

'Best and most regular boys' at the National School, Treherbert are rewarded by having their photograph taken, 19 July 1900.

Staff at Treherbert Infants School, 1913.

Class 1A at Treherbert Infants School, 1913.

A well-ordered and seemingly disciplined class at Treherbert Infants School, 1926. Everyone is looking at the camera – quite an achievement!

Pupils at Treherbert Senior Boys' School, 1936.

The official opening of Treherbert Cottage Hospital, 7 December 1927. The Chairman of the Hospital Committee was Mr Trefor L. Mort ME, JP.

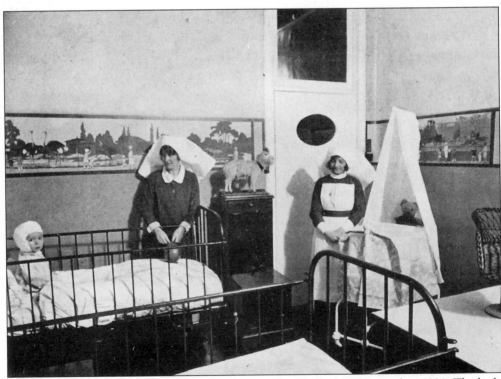

Matron Morris and a nurse in the Alice Beynon ward at Treherbert Hospital, c. 1931. The little girl is Valerie Green from Garden Village, Tynewydd (Roger Green's daughter). She is now living at No 10 Dumfries Street, Treorchy.

Treherbert Cymric Party, 1925. From left to right, back row: W. Davies, T.J. Davies, D. Parsons, J.I. Jones, I.L. Jones, G. Hugh, W.M. Owen, J. Owen, W. Roberts, T.G. Owen, D. Rees. Middle row: I. Elms, M. Rosser, T. Griffiths, R. Jenkins, I. John, G. Lodwig, H. Fletcher, W. Harris, D. Jones, J.B. Jones, B. Roberts, I. Jones, I.G. Owen. Front row: G. Griffiths, D. Jones, B. Owen (Secretary), E.T. Jones (Chairman), J. Owen (conductor), T.L. Davies ME (President), Dr D.C. Williams (Vice-President), Miss E. Hugh LLCM (accompanist), L. Lewis (Treasurer), C. Lodwig, G. James. Seated on the floor: G. Howells, Master Hedley Davies, P.R. Owen. Dai Parsons remembers that the club was formed in the mid-1920s. It existed solely for its choir work and only performed locally. Practice was held in a building, probably council-owned, at the top of Taff Street, Treherbert.

Treherbert Dandy Holiday Club and Debating Society (combined) was formed *c*. 1905. The members are pictured here in 1932.

Officers of the Treherbert Lodge (No 33) of the Loyal Order of Moose, 1932. From left to right, insets: Owen Evans, -?-, -?-, Sid Miles, Back row: Sydney John, -?-, David Davies ('Dai Gwas'), William J. Thomas (butcher), -?-, -?-, -?-, Ivor Idris Jones, -?-, -?-. Middle row: Peter Davies (outfitter, with light-coloured collar). Front row: H.J. Wood, -?-, Morgan Williams (teacher), W.E. 'Potty' Pearce (with glasses), -?-, -?-.

Treherbert Co-operative Guild, 1928. From left to right, back row: Mrs Peach, Mrs Thomas, Mrs Cory, Mrs Evans, Mrs Jones. Front row: Mrs Waits, Mrs Francis, -?-, -?-. On the floor: Mrs Sivell and Mrs Jenkins.

Treherbert Hospital Queen Ceridwen Platt (*née* Jones), *c*. 1936.

Treherbert railway station, *c*. 1912. The line on the left side of the platform was the Swansea line; the Cardiff line was on the right. The turntable can be seen on the curved line on the right of the photograph. Lady Margaret Colliery is in the background.

'Egbert' the Tank pictured in Station Street, Treherbert. Such tanks were used in national tours by the government during the First World War to court public enthusiasm for bonds needed to help fund the war effort.

Treherbert Home Guard, 1942. Among those pictured: Sylvanus Thompson, Jack Lewis, Morgan Jones, Teifi Davies, Frank Vickery, Dai Griffiths, Gwynfi Jones, Dewi Lewis, Percy Evans, Dick Merry, Dilwyn Jones, Tudor Williams, Frank Reade, Sid Miles (Captain), Dewi Edwards, Frank Hoffman.

Dressed up to celebrate the end of the Second World War, Upper Taff Street, Treherbert. From left to right, back row: Mrs Thomas, John Rowsell, Mrs MacMillan, -?-. Front row: -?- Mrs Poole, Enid Bembow, Hilary Pomeroy.

Minister and members of Libanus Chapel, Treherbert, 1949. *Gweinidog a swyddogion Libanus.* From left to right, back row: Nicholas Jones, R. Prysor Williams, James Owen, J.L. Haddock, Dewi O. Evans. Second row: Miss B. Williams BA, Mrs P. Harris, Mrs A. Pryse Williams, Miss B. Evans, Miss P. Jones, Miss C. Jones, Mrs E. Jones, Miss R.A. Griffiths. Front row: Mrs K. Fletcher, Miss L. Cule, Parch. D. Pryse Williams, Mrs J. Hugh, Mrs E. Jones.

Members of Horeb Chapel, Treherbert who took part (c. 1935) in a play performed at the Prince of Wales Theatre in Cardiff for the National Eisteddfod being held in the city. From left to right, back row: Lizzie Jones, Annie Jenkins, Prysor Williams, Bessie Evans, -?-, Hannah Williams, -?-. Front row: -?-, Beck Price, Dilys Davies, Susie Jones.

Nativity play at St Mary's Church, *c.* 1942.

Wesleyan 50/50 Club annual dinner, *c.* 1956. From left to right, standing: Jimmy Lloyd, Ernie Fair, Jack Williams, Ron Jones, Roy Green. Sitting clockwise around the table: Enid Benbow, John Scott, Freda Williams, Cecil Pritchard, Muriel Lloyd, -?- (glasses), Tom Phelps, Jim Phelps, Dora Phelps, Brian Fews, Jean Phelps.

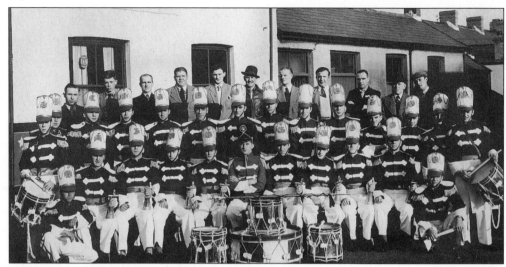

Treherbert Toy Drum Majors outside the Railway Bar (their headquarters), *c.* 1950. Johnny Gowan is the drum major, Des Rees is on side drum to the left, George Fisher is fourth from the right in the front row and Bill Davies, who was drill and formation instructor and treasurer, is fourth from the right in the back row. Practice took place twice a week and the band was the only one in South Wales to win a competition against the Aberfan Coons.

Treherbert Silver Band at the National Eisteddfod, Caerffili, *c.* 1955. Among those pictured, from left to right, back row: John O'Leary, Pete Eddy, Phil Broome, Eddy White … Fred Prior (conductor) … T. Pickens, … ? Bateman, … Jimmy May, Gary Williams, Alan Pickens, Pete Eddy, Danny Morris, Horace Bigfield. Front row: … Myrddin Jakeman, Ron Thomas, ? Eddy, ? Eddy.

St Mary's Church Sunday school concert – *The Sylvan Queen* – held in Bethany schoolroom, 1952. From left to right, back row: -?-, Sonia Scott, Olive Harris, Marion White, Vera Jenkins, -?-, Harold Austin, Thelma Sweet, -?-, -?-, Jean Black, Margaret Jones, Karen Matthews, Mrs Harris, -?-, -?-, Sylvia Chapelle, David Hunt, Keith Doughty, Pat Thomas, Will Williams, Betty Williams. Fourth row: Rev Austin Lewis (Vicar), Mrs Thomas, Mrs Rose, John Walters, Michael Watkins, Keith Thomas (clown), -?-, Dennis Rose, Joan West, Billy Edwards, Maureen Thomas, -?-, Doreen Bateman, -?-, -?-, Megan Husband, Ada Doughty, Ron Jenkins (curate). Third row: Peter Berry, Ann White, Ann Bowen. Second row: David Jenkins, Neil Willis, -?-, Joan Hunt, -?-, -?-, -?-, -?-, -?-, -?-, Glenys Broome, Irene Hunt, -?-, -?-, -?-, Roger Thomas, Handel Rich. Front row: Len Pearce, Elizabeth Roberts, -?-, -?-, Susan Thomas, Eileen Rose, -?-, -?-, -?-, Marion Rose, -?-, -?-, -?-, -?-, -?-, Tony Willis, Billy Harris.

St Mary's Church Sunday school concert, 1955, also held in the Bethany schoolroom. From left to right, back row: Mrs Rose, Betty Williams, Shirley Douglas, Marion Hicks, -?-, -?-, -?-, -?-, -?-, Margaret Howells, Ronald Thomas, -?-, -?-, -?-. Third row: Vicar Lewis, Mrs Thomas, Vivienne Howley, Harold Austin (Choirmaster). Second row: -?-, -?-, -?-, Ann Bowen, Gerwyn Llewellyn, Dave Howley, Ann Parry, Will Williams, Margaret Jones, -?-, -?-, Marion Rose, -?-, Harry Rose. Front row: Idris Thomas (6th from left), Robert Thomas (7th), Terry McGovern (8th), Peter Berry (9th), David Jones (10th), David Lewis (11th), Susan Thomas (far right).

Official opening of the Old Age Pensioners' Hall in Treherbert, 15 May 1958. From left to right: Tom Thomas (Tyglas), Tom Anfield (on chair), -?-, Mr Evans (Mayor of Rhondda), Mrs Broome, Mrs Hayes, Annie May Jones, Mrs Morgan, Mrs Edwards, -?-. The partially-covered face of the man back right belongs to Rev D. Young.

Dr Griffith John Hughes MD, FRCS (Edin.) was born on the Llŷn peninsula in North Wales. He studied medicine at Edinburgh University and afterwards took up a practice at Rosyth, later working at the Edinburgh Royal Infirmary. In 1930, an uncle, Dr Edward Hughes, who had been working at Pentre, wrote to him, following the death of Dr D.C. Williams, regarding the vacant practice in Treherbert linked to the Ynysfeio Colliery. By the time of his retirement in 30 June 1965 Dr Hughes was calling at over 800 houses in the district, extending from Blaencwm and Blaenrhondda down to Gelli and Ystrad. He was a staunch supporter of the cause at Horeb Welsh Presbyterian Chapel, where he was an elder for many years.

TESTIMONIAL FUND :-: 1965

——::——

PRESENTATION MEETING

by

PATIENTS and FRIENDS

for

Dr. G. J. HUGHES
M.D., F.R.C.S. (Edin.)

and

Mr. F. HOCKADAY
(Medical Dispenser)

at

**HOREB CHAPEL, TREHERBERT
ON WEDNESDAY, 1st DECEMBER, 1965**

——::——

Musical Entertainment provided by :
THE TREORCHY MALE VOICE CHOIR

Conductor : Mr. JOHN DAVIES, M.B.E.

Accompanist : Mr. TOM JONES

with Supporting Artistes

Chairman : Councillor J. H. LEWIS

SOUVENIR PROGRAMME

1930 - 1965

Prysor Williams acted on radio with the BBC Repertory Company performing in both English and Welsh-language plays. He is seen here in *Y Darn Arian* (A Piece of Silver) transmitted on BBC Television on 24 January 1961. From left to right: Brinley Williams (as Cardotyn), Prysor Williams (as Y Gŵr), Rachel Thomas (as Y Wraig). Prysor also acted on the big screen in the films *The Last Days of Dolwyn* with Richard Burton, *Only Two Can Play* with Peter Sellers and *The Blue Scar*.

Arnold's grocer's shop, Bute Street, 1955. From left to right: Martin Griffiths, T.J. Arnold, Beryl Parker, Mavis Davies.

Bute Square, Treherbert, *c*. 1938.

Bute Street, Treherbert, *c*. 1953.

William Todd Duncan (on right with his block marked WTD) at Bute Colliery, c. 1938. Will was called up in the Second World War, although he was a collier, because he was in the St John Ambulance. He joined the Royal Army Medical Corps and was killed in 1940.

A derelict Lady Margaret Colliery looking towards Penyrenglyn, c. 1950. On the right-hand side of the picture is the huge colliery tip which is now the Baglan playing field. In the background is the Ynysfeio Colliery.

Looking over the derelict Lady Margaret Colliery towards Treherbert, *c.* 1950. In the centre left of picture is the white-faced Gaiety Cinema and on the mountainside is St Mary's Church.

Treherbert Shrapnel RFC, winners of the District League and Knock-out Competition, 1920.

Treherbert RFC, 1928-29 season. From left to right, back row: J. Davies (Treasurer), W. Davies, E. Evans, H. Shore, D. Lewis, H. Davies, D. Morgan, G. Williams, G. Hursh. Second row, seated: J. Preece, H. Evans, W. Jones (Secretary), G. Parry (Captain), H. Wall (Chairman), R. Watkins, T. Parry. Front row: S. Harris (squatting), M. Williams, W. Morris, E. Jenkins, S. Jones, W. Morris. In 1893 Treherbert RFC were playing on what was called the Picnic Field, now Treherbert Park. In 1895 they moved to Ynysfelin Field and played their last game there in the 1928-29 season, the team for which is pictured above. The field was taken over by the Great Western Railway who built engine sheds there. The site is now occupied by the Everest double-glazing factory.

Tennis players at Treherbert Park, c. 1930. From left to right: Mr Leason (dentist), Trevor Sheriden, Cllr Rhys Morgan Rhys, Jack Bryn Jones, Eddie Thomas (Wine Stores).

Treherbert bowls team, *c.* 1935. From left, back row: Mr Eveleigh (5th); middle row: George Payne (2nd), Mr Davies (4th), Mr Arnold (6th); front row: Mr Gruar (3rd), Michael Davies (holding the shield), Bob Evans (6th).

Opening day at Treherbert's outdoor swimming pool, 1936. This was demolished in 1994 and a new indoor pool was built on the same site.

Treherbert Penguins junior water-polo team, 1948. From left to right, back row: John Morris, John Broughton, Alwyn Evans, Ieuan ?. Front row: Ron Collins, Emrys Jenkins, Ron Green. With the ball: Kevin Jones.

Treherbert Youth Club rounders team, 1952-53. From left to right, back row: Nanw Stanton, -?-, -?-. Front row: Tom Jones, Moira Harris, Shirley Watts, Mair Jones, -?-, Sheila Evans, Harry Corfield.

Treherbert Boys Club basketball team, 1960. From left to right, back row: E. Jenkins, B. Murphy, Gary Glover, Roger Cope, Paul Barclay, Haydn Bundock, Jim Owen. Front row: David Thomas, Brian Rees, Len Pearce, Adrian ?.

Treherbert RFC, 1961-62 season. From left to right, back row: Viv Price, Pete Smith, Adrian Thomas, Joe Barclay. Third row: Michael Watts, Gerwyn Llewellyn, Vic Townsend, Alan Jones, Ron Rees, Myrddin Pearce, Tommy Morgan, Gwyn Davies, Parry Williams, Tom Cullen, Gwyn Rees, -?-, Malcolm Thomas. Second row: Peter Davies, Elwyn Buckland, Kevin Jones, Brian Peasley, Ron Jones, Len Howells, Peter White. Front row: Gwyn Jones, Alan Jones, Tudor Parry, Robert Griffiths (schoolboy international), -?-, Brian James, Mike Holleyfield.

'Hair Style and Colour Show' presented by Glenise Hair Fashions of Treherbert in co-operation with Clairol at the Polikoff's club, Pentre on 1 March 1967. From left to right: Gillian Hinton, Lynne Jackson, Esme Phillips, Marion Williams, Judith Davies, Evelyn Jones.

Sonia Ross from Birmingham, Beauty Queen of Britain, 1967 modelling at the 'Hair Style and Colour Show'. Seated to the left of Miss Ross is Mrs Nellie May Howard of Gwalia Galleries. On her right is Mrs Marged Ann Williams.

Five

Tynewydd

Blaencwm Sunday school, Tynewydd, c. 1900. *Dosbarth Ysgol Sul Blaencwm.*

Garden village (now Castleton Avenue), *c.* 1920. The road leading away to the right went to Fernhill Houses.

General view of Tynewydd, *c.* 1925.

The butcher's shop at No 28 Wyndham Street, Tynewydd, *c*. 1912. Mrs Jane Llewellyn and her daughter Margaret Ann are pictured.

Looking across Tynewydd towards Blaenrhondda, *c*. 1945. Hope Chapel – now Tynewydd surgery – is the building in the centre.

Staff at Dunraven School, 1913. Fifth from the left in the middle row is Myfanwy Prosser the headmistress. Fifth from the left in the front row is May Reynolds, head of infants.

Standard 4 at Dunraven Girls' School, 1913.

Edwin, Haydn and Donald Bundock (left to right) outside their home at No 4 Upper St Albans Road, Tynewydd, 1927.

Ieuan, John and Peter Lazarus (left to right) outside No 22 Wyndham Street, 1933. Their home was next-door to Bennet's ironmongers, part of which can be seen on the right of the picture. Note the washing board in the window.

Class 1 at Dunraven Infants' School, July 1931.

Dunraven Boys' School, championship winners at Treherbert Hospital School Sports, Ward I, 1927.

Class 4 at Dunraven Infants' School, July 1931.

Children at Dunraven Infants' School, 1936.

Members of Blaencwm Chapel, *c.* 1934. From left to right, back row: Ivor Williams, Desmond Lynton, Emrys Owen, John Haydn Davies, David Williams, Henry Shepherd, John Cook, G. Griffiths. Front row: Sally Williams, Nell Edwards, Thomas Owen, Megan Price, Beck Davies.

Class at Dunraven Junior (Mixed) School, 1963-64. From left to right, back row: Howard Neal, Alan Davies, Robert Aldritch, Richard Moon, Jeffrey Green, Gary Jones, Philip Green, David Griffiths, Gerald Read, Peter Davies. Second row: Mary Pritchard, Robert Thomas, Gary Medcraft, Reg Carpenter, -?-, -?-. Front row: Margaret Cook, Carol Francis, Susan Mason, Susan Lee, Lynne John, Meryl Evans, Alison Beauchamp, Linda Smart, Karen Coleman, Susan Bailey.

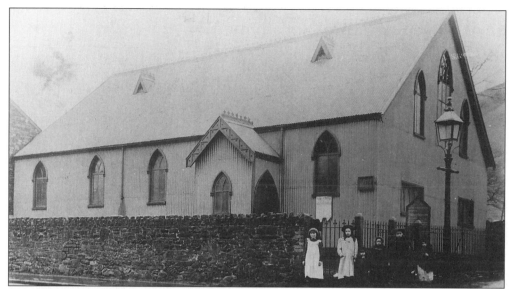

Soar Welsh Baptist Chapel, Tynewydd, *c.* 1908.

Members of Soar Chapel dressed for a performance of *Snow White and the Seven Dwarfs*, 1939. The photograph was taken in the grounds of Tynewydd Cottage. From left to right, back row: - ?-, Doreen Smart, Cyril Pratt, Vera Williams, Mona Williams, Ieuan Lazarus, Lil Thomas. Second row: Malcolm Griffiths, Ron Pritchard, Roy Jones, Gary Williams, Gwilym Parfitt. Front row: Des Barnett, -?-.

Upper Rhondda Orchestra, 1920.

The Ambassadors Dance Orchestra which played in the Tynewydd Labour Club's Lido dance-hall in the late 1930s and 1940s. From left to right, back row: ? Jones, Tom Jenkins ('Tippit'), Bob Green, Cyril (known as 'Al') Fox, Haydn Brazell. Front row: Morgan Richards, -?-, Tom Carpenter, Will Harding, Ben Thomas.

The prize-winning Green and Whites Star and Crescent Band, pictured outside Treherbert Hospital, 1953. Among those pictured, left to right, from the back: Megan Chidgey, Val Watts, Phyllis Adams, Mel Rawlins, Ellen Pugh, Marion Pugh, Marie Thomas, Peggy Thomas, Nesta Bishop, Freda Biggs, Jane Evans, Betty Moon, Betty Lazarus, Glenys Fisher, Llew Bailey, Olwen Cook, Muriel Rawlins, Enid Evans, Pop Lee, Lewis Thomas, John Morgan, Gwyn Williams, Ivor Davies, Jack Thomas, Gary Williams, Ron Rees.

Newspaper article on the popular Tynewydd Labour Club and the individual driving forces behind it, mid-1950s.

Gay in the Rhondda

RHONDDA'S largest club is the Tynewydd Labour Club at Treherbert. It has a membership of 1,210 and has a waiting list of would-be members which has steadily grown since the books were closed a few years ago.

Founded in 1912, it is a busy club. Steward and Stewardess Mr. and Mrs. Cyril Jones have five bar assistants to meet the demands of members.

A feature of the club is the large concert hall—"The Lido" —very much in demand for dances and other functions. The club hopes soon to spend £30,000-£40,000 on renovations to this hall.

For the annual children's outing 45 double-decker buses are needed each summer to convey members, their wives and some 750 children to the seaside. Each child receives 15s. pocket money for the day.

There is always something on at the club, and in recent years it has become a popular rendezvous.

The club is to provide all the curtains at the local O.A.P. centre. A piano has already been presented to the centre.

Trevor Roderick.—Secretary for past four years. Like all the club officers he is a life member. He was a trade union official for some 30 years.

Tom Harris. — Chairman from 1943 to 1948, he was employed as steward from 1948 to 1953. He then resigned and was again elected to the chair last year.

Albert Hambury.—Treasurer for 35 years. A 75-year-old retired miner, he worked for 58 years underground — only missing one day. On that day he was loading timber ON TOP of the colliery.

Tom Johns. — Assistant secretary for 17 years. Aged 73 years, Tom is a retired mason. He has been a member for 36 years.

Cyril Jones.—Steward. He took over duties from the present chairman and is a former miner.

William Richards.—Always called "Mr." Richards by the younger members, he is 81. A retired miner, he is the grandfather of Ross Richards, the Aberavon R.F.C. full-back.

Glyn Jones. — Librarian. Over 100 books are borrowed weekly. Proud that library contains modern and complete Encyclopaedia Britannica (cost £95). He was the club secretary from 1917 to 1918.

95

TYNEWYDD HOTEL, ASSEMBLY ROOMS

A GRAND BOXING SHOW

will be held at the above place

On Monday, December 19th, 1927,

when the following Bouts will be Staged—

8 2-min. Round Contest between PHINEAS JOHN (who can be backed for £25 against any 7st 10lbs lad in the Country) & HAYDN JONES, Penygraig (a lad who makes them fight every inch of way

6 2-min. Contest between DAVE GRACE, Penygraig and GEORGE WILLIAMS, Treherbert

Also, OTHER EXHIBITION BOUTS.

M.C.—Mr. LEWIS PARRY   Referee—Mr. BRYN DAVIES
Timekeeper—Mr. TOMMY DAVIES

Boxing to commence at 7 o'clock sharp.

Tickets   -   6d
Emlyn Office, Treorchy

Ticket for a boxing bout held at the Tynewydd Hotel (known popularly as 'The Bricks'), 19 December 1927.

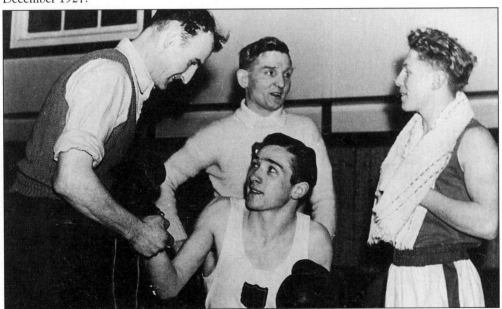

Members of the Fernhill Amateur Boxing Club who trained in the Fernhill Working Men's Institute under the Palace Cinema in Tynewydd, 1950. From left to right: Jack Pritchard (committee member), George Smith (trainer), Emlyn Jones and Mal Sampson (boxers). Emlyn was the NCB National champion in 1951 and also a three-time finalist at the ABA Championships and Welsh champion on a few occasions. He later became a member of the Mines Rescue Brigade based at Dinas. Mal was a Welsh flyweight champion and British Army Cadet and British All Star champion. He now keeps a greengrocer's shop in Bute Street, Treorchy.

The Evie Davies Quintet at the Tynewydd Labour Club, 1944. Three of the band members were Tommy French, Bob Green (drums), Evie Davies (sax). Others pictured include Walter Locket, Gwynfor Evans, Alwyn Evans, John Morgan, Eileen Locket, Dilys Evans, Gweno Evans, Jean Morgan, Bob Morgan.

The Basini family who ran a shop in Wyndham Square, c. 1950. From left to right: Jack Basini, daughter Mary, Mrs Basini, daughter Rene.

Twins Jeffrey and Philip Green on their father's motor-cycle at the back of No 42 Eileen Place, Tynewydd, 1957.

Tynewydd cricket team, *c.* 1950. From left to right, back row: Lyn Williams, Dai Rees, Arthur J. Davies, ? Watts, Dorion Rees, Elwyn Jones, Gary Evans. Front row: Charlie Williams, ? Gale, -?-, Morlais Adams, John Jones, Graham Phillips, Don Parfitt.

The open area of land, centre (pictured c. 1945) was known as Eileen Park, as it was situated at the end of Eileen Place. It was entered via the bridge on the right of picture. Behind the 'Carlton' truck, between the two sets of lines, can be seen an area of stagnant water. After heavy rain this 'pond' used to become about 3ft deep and children would play pirates there using railway sleepers as ships. During soccer games on the field it was an honoured task to retrieve the ball when it had been kicked into the river. A colander-shaped net fixed to the end of a long pole was used and it was quite a hard and risky task if the river was in full spate. During the summer the Tynewydd Cricket Club used Eileen Park for matches. They played on a thick coconut mat about 8ft wide. It was considered a privilege amongst local boys to be allowed to roll up the mat at the end of the game and carry it to the cricket shed. It was a heavy job requiring about six boys.

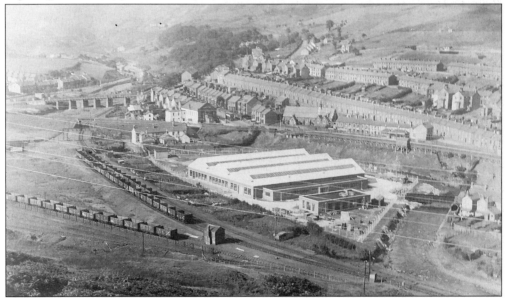

By 1958 the Rollo Hardy Tubular Steel Factory had been built on the site of Eileen Park.

Miskin Street party held to celebrate the Investiture of the Prince of Wales in 1969. From left to right, standing: Marion Williams, Elwyn Rees, Randal Cory, Lydia Cory, -?-, -?-, Joan Green, Barbara Ware, -?-, Maisie Longhurst. At the table facing the camera are Paul Ware, Roger Green, Denise Green and Mary Cope.

Dai Jenkins of Victoria Street competing in the 1993 fun run organised by the Rhondda Cancer Care charity group and the Rhondda Valley Runners. This annual run starts at the top of the Treherbert to Rhigos road and takes the runners along forestry tracks, skirting the Lluest Wen dam, emerging back on the Treherbert Road below Tycoedca farm before ending on the rugby field.

Six
Blaenrhondda

Blacksmith's shop at the rear of No 118 Brook Street, c. 1910. From left to right: William John Richards, Iori Davies (grandson), Timothy Davies (son), -?- (in doorway), Thomas Davies (grandson), Jonah Davies (grandson), William Timothy Davies (father and owner of the smithy); he was popularly known as 'Tim-y-gof'.

Smokestack at Fernhill Colliery, c. 1914.

Engine derailment below Fernhill Colliery, c. 1895. Was it pushed, shoved or frightened off the line by the man with his hands in his pockets!?

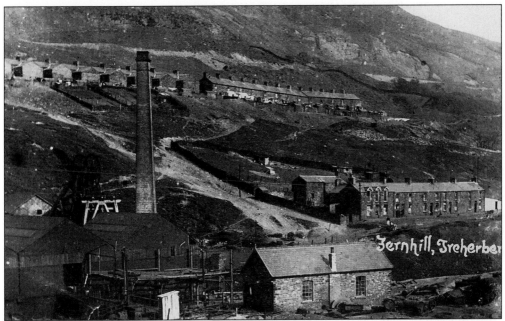

No 1 pit at Fernhill Colliery, *c.* 1950. The building in the foreground is the lamp-room. The houses on the right are 'Office Row' and the gabled building was the home of the farrier Mr Dutton at this time, with Mrs Pearce at No 2, Mrs Thomas (No 3), Mrs Keating (No 4) and Bob Morgans (No 5). This terrace was demolished in July 1962 and Fernhill Houses (in the background) in 1963-64.

Fernhill workmen outside the pit-top lodge, No 3 shaft, at the end of a day-shift in 1944. Some of the men present were: George Noble, Don Davies, Bert Sealey, Will Morris, John Lazarus, Cyril Bishop, Trevor Binding, Alan Evans, Clive Baker, Harry Powell, Em Worral, Ray Pate, Bryn Cole, Tom Worral.

Fernhill Colliery Consultative Committee, c. 1945. From left to right, back row: Evan Williams, Cyril Rees, -?-, -?-, Morgan Jones, Jack Pratt, D.J. Hughes. Front row: John ('Shony') Davies, Trevor Roderick, Mr Oliver, Ron Jones, Len Fitzpatrick, D.J. Davies.

Underground visit by Fernhill Colliery canteen staff, 1952. From left to right: Albert Fox (colliery manager), Connie Lewis, Murina Jenkins, -?-, -?-, -?-, Florrie Fisher, Mary Lewis, Charles Jenkins (unit electrical engineer)

Fernhill Colliery pit-head baths attendants pictured in the showers section, 1958. From left to right: Walter Phelps, Ron John, Gwilym Thomas, Ormond Vaughan, Arthur Morris.

Fernhill Colliery fire-fighting team, winners of the National Coal Board's Area 3 fire-fighting competition in 1964. From left to right, back row: Henry Coram, Islwyn Jones, Gwyn Phillips, Ionawr Richards, Terry Collinson. Front row: -?-, Fred Woods, Dai John Hughes (manager), Bob Berry, Roy Green.

Fernhill rescue team with their wives, at an annual dinner at Driscoll's Restaurant in Porth, 1967. From left to right, back row: Dorion Hart, Bob Berry, Gwyn Phillips, Islwyn Morgan, Gwilym Davies, Dorion Rees. Front row: Julie Phillips, Janice Hart, Margaret Berry, -?-, Mair Davies, Phyllis Morgan, Doris Butler, Dilwyn Butler.

Fernhill Colliery, c. 1950. Nos 5, 4 and 3 shafts are in the foreground, the washery is behind No 5 headgear, which is the nearest. On the left-hand side of the railway track Nos 2 and 1 shafts can be seen. On the mountainside are Fernhill Houses.

Members of Fernhill NUM Lodge Committee at the South Wales Miners' Gala, held annually in Cardiff, c. 1975. In the foreground are Les Hill, Cliff True, Mary Lewis, Dai Clements, Harry Pearce, Don Bundock and Keith Barnes.

Unveiling ceremony at the War Memorial in Clyngwyn Road erected in the 1920s to commemorate the men who had lost their lives in the First World War.

Blaenrhondda football team, *c.* 1921.

Football field at the rear of Caroline Street, the last street on the left-hand side of Blaenrhondda going up the valley.

Blaenrhondda Cricket Club, *c.* 1946. From left to right: William Henry Williams, Ken Carpenter, Morgan Rees, Ike Perkins, Tom Beard, Mansel Williams, Alec Lewis, Tom ('Tosh') Rees, -?-, Jonah Davies, Jim Mears, -?-.

Blaenrhondda Boys' Club soccer team, 1936-37. From left to right, back row: ? Griffiths, Haydn Bundock, Dil Davies, Gwyn Williams, Charlie Gardner, Idris Bowden, George Thorner, ? Pearce. Middle row: ? Thomas, William ('Froggy') Powell, Tom Bryant, Basil John, Trevor Lewis, Jack Williams, Chris Phillips. Front row: Glan Williams, Will ('Dougie') Rees, Evie John, Lewin Withers, Joe Roberts.

Blaenrhondda School dancers, *c.* 1960. From left to right: Mair Gardner, Mair Jones, Teg Thomas, Marion Thomas.

Blaenrhondda Juvenile Choir, 1918.

Blaenrhondda United Choir, pictured in 1935 to celebrate their golden jubilee. Their conductor was J. Samlet Jones.

Fernhill workmen, on holiday from the pit in 1950. They had travelled to Truro, Cornwall to spend their break on farms picking potatoes. From left to right, back row: Jack Demaid, Will Johnson, Dicky Broome, Tommy Morgan. Front row: Harry Pearce, Haydn Parfitt, Don Bundock, Dai Morgan, John Pearce.

Standard 7 at Blaenrhondda School, 1930.

Street party in Caroline Street to celebrate the Coronation of King George VI in 1937. Seated in the front of the picture are Jack Hawkins, -?-, Tom Carpenter and Cyril Lewis. Note Fernhill Colliery stable in the background.

Blaenrhondda Special Police, 'G' Division (Glam.), 1945. From left to right, back row: S/C D.C. Jones, S/C R. Demaid, S/C B.C. Seeley, S/C F. White. Front row: S/C J. Davies, S/Sgt G. Broome, PC Broughton, S/Insp. A. Demaid, S/C J. Demaid.

Blaenrhondda Youth Club, pictured in Blaenrhondda School, 1950. The teacher is Charlie Evans (far left of front row).

Members of the Tabernacle Sunday school commemorating the gift of a clock (on the wall) in 1956 by Philip Rees Thomas who had emigrated to Pittsburgh, Pennsylvania, USA. From left to right, back row: William Llewellyn, Stephen John, William John Owen, David Rees, Gerwyn Llewellyn, -?-, Randall Wilkins, William John Richards, Teifi Davies, Ron John, Betty Dear, Bernard Dear, Marion Morgan, Avril Davies. Second row: David Ross Davies, Gwilym Davies, Len Coles, Myrddin Davies, Siân Davies, Sharon Davies, Angela Woodward, Ann Lewis, Meryl Rees, Carol Davies. Front row: Phil Edwards, David John, Rowena Morgan, Annette Morgan, Eleanor Lee, Susan Demaid, Christine Davies, Ron Davies, Pauline Davies.

Pupils at Blaenrhondda School, 1959-60. From left to right, back row: Terence Dury, Malcolm Davies, Roly Price, Philip Llewellyn, Dudley Jenkins, Alan Morris, Ken Poole, Victor Carpenter, Alan John Davies. Third row: David Roberts, Steven John, Keith Melyn, Philip Harris, Alan Bishop, Graham Roberts, Gaynor Stanton, Brenda Spurway, Marion Griffiths. Second row: Linda Spurrey, Janice Davies (who later became headmistress of the school), Annette Rees, Pat Pascoe, Janice Eynon, Jean Thomas, Janet Brooks, Ann Williams, Gwyneth Jones. Front row: Linda Bailey, Rhylla Thomas, Lynne Jones, Carol Davies, Mary Lewis. The teacher to the left is Alan Griffiths with Mr Thomas the headmaster on the right.

After very heavy rain in 1960, tip movement on the Fernhill Colliery site blocked the river at the entrance to the lower part of the culvert thereby causing the river to flow down the railway line, past the colliery screens to the top of Blaenrhondda and then through the village.

The landlord and his family outside the Blaenrhondda Hotel ('The Kick'), c. 1908. From left to right: Thomas, Elizabeth, John Davies senior (landlord), Mary, Naomi (mother), John ('Jack').

The retirement of Wilf Fussel as landlord of the Blaenrhondda Hotel ('The Kick'). From left to right, back row: Dewi Griffiths, Tom Hayward, -?-, Gilly Edwards. Middle 'row': Ned Davies, Graham Mears, Ivor Holder. Front: Newton Sampson, Nancy Holder, Anita Holder, Jim Squires, Arthur Morris (making the presentation), -?-, Frank Donovan, Ivor Watts, Wilf Fussel.

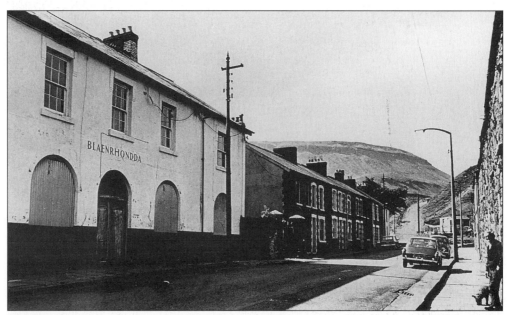

The Blaenrhondda Hotel was demolished in 1976. The man standing opposite is Will Richards, known locally as Will 'Fish'. The track at the back of the picture led to the No 1 and No 2 shafts of Fernhill Colliery.

Seven

Blaencwm

Teaching staff at Blaencwm School, *c.* 1910.

Mr John David, first General Manager of the Rhondda & Swansea Bay Railway. This line ran a distance of 24 miles and 31 chains. Work commenced in 1882 and was completed in 1899. This included the enormous task of digging the Blaencwm to Blaengwynfi Tunnel which is 1 mile, 1,683 yards long.

Signal box on the Rhondda & Swansea Bay Railway line on the Blaencwm side of the tunnel to Blaengwynfi. Engine drivers picked up a key from the signal box each side before travelling through the tunnel.

Company officials at Glenrhondda Colliery, Blaencwm, *c*. 1936. Second from the right is Harry Hughes, colliery cashier.

A view down the valley taken in the 1950s showing, on the left, the main railway line leading to Blaenrhondda and Treherbert stations and, on the right, part of Glenrhondda Colliery including the coal screens.

Diesel train leaving Blaencwm Tunnel, late 1950s.

BLAENCWM, NEAR TREHERBERT.

W.5656.

Blaencwm, c. 1940. The Glenrhondda Colliery is in the centre of picture and the railway tunnel is on its right.

Tydraw House, Blaencwm, *c.* 1951. At that time the colliery mechanic lived in the left-hand wing and the manager in the main house. On the extreme right was Tydraw Farm. The house is now the residence of the retired Dr Walter Williams.

Glenrhondda Colliery Working Men's Institute, 1923.

Soup kitchen organised by Blaencwm Distress Committee during the 1921 lock-out of the miners. From left to right, back row: Ernie Frowen, Lewis Jones, Harold Evans, Will ('Digger') Wessendorf, George Berry. Front row: Evan Phillips, Mrs Jones, -?-, -?-, Mrs Davies ('Dal'), Mrs Parry, William Lisle.

Blaencwm, c. 1950. The concrete wall on the extreme right of picture (at the end of Dilys Street) was demolished after the flood of 27 December 1979.

The undermanager of Glenrhondda Colliery with his first car, purchased for £13 in 1958.

Glenrhondda Colliery, 1959.

Committee and Trustees of Tydraw Workmen's Institute, 1948-49. From left to right, back row: F. Cook, S. Lazarus, T. Evans, E. Jones, L. Curry, E. Jones, E. Coles, P. Griffiths (caretaker), S. Jones (1948 Chairman). Front row: J. Saunders (Trustee), T. Anfield (Trustee), T. Rees (Vice-Chairman), D.S. Evans ME (Trustee), T.J. Davies ME (1949 Chairman), D.J. Thomas (Secretary), J. Jenkins. The Institute was opened in January 1920 by Sir Clifford Cory MP who defrayed half the cost of the building and contributed £50 towards the furnishing of the library. The front of the building is of Forest of Dean stone. The architect was W.D. Morgan, Pentre, the contractor, Charles Jenkins & Sons, Porth and the cost of the building, £1,000.

Tydraw Colliery annual dance, Treherbert Conservative Club, 1950. From left to right, back row: Mrs Thomas, Abe Henry, Lil King, Harry Cull, Will Hart, Islwyn Phillips, Morgan Jones, Will Jones, Don Ruddock, Danny Fitzgerald, Ivor Roles, -?-, Joe Parker, Glyn Grant, Glyn Lisle. Second 'row': Mrs Cull, -?-, -?-, -?-, Mrs Davies, Mrs Williams (with glasses), Haydn Davies, Dai Williams, Betty Nicholas, Linda Lisle, Will Nicholas, Roy Green, Mavis Green, Trevor King, Will Jones, May Evans, -?-, Jack Rees, -?-, Charlie Thomas, Cyril Smart, -?-, Bryn Lisle, Walt Murray. Seated: Will Skerm, Mrs Skerm, Will Lewis, Mrs Rees, -?-.

Blaencwm school meals service, *c*. 1963. Ivor Watts is on the left.

Presentation supper for five retiring miners, Glenrhondda Colliery, *c*. 1961. From left to right, back row: Ned Rees, Will Brunker, Wally Evans, Jack Thomas, Cliff Hobbs, Gordon Rogers, -?-, Dai Lock, D. Rees, Stan Dean, Alf Scott. Front row: Fred Green -?-, -?-, Dai Williams, Jack Duggan.

Tom Carpenter's Arcadian Harmonica Band, 1941. From left to right, back row: Iris Anfield, Will Morris, Cyril Peachy, John Price, -?-, Arthur Bugler, Ben Jackson, -?-, Tom Carpenter. Front row: Dai Will Griffiths, -?-, Bert Ruddock, Tom Morgan, Sylvanus Thompson, Jack Lewis. In front of the drums: Peggy Spiller and Gwyn Jenkins.

Blaencwm children, *c.* 1925.

Blaencwm School, 1955. The headmaster was John Haydn Davies.

Children at Blaencwm School, 1958. Included in the photo are teacher Mrs S. Jenkins, sister-in-law to Richard Burton; headmaster John Haydn Davies, conductor of Treorchy Male Voice Choir and, third from the right in the back row, playwright Frank Vickery.

Acknowledgements

The authors would like to thank a large number of individuals and organisations for their help in the compilation of this book. Without their assistance it would not have been possible to present the photographic history of the area in all its rich variety. We sincerely apologise to anyone who has helped us over the years if they have been inadvertently omitted from the following list.

Louie Balestrazzi, Edna Barnes, Margaret Berry, Blaencwm School, Blaenrhondda School, Haydn Bundock, Gwilym Davies, Gwyn Davies, John Davies, Teifi Davies, Wynford Duggan, Roy Duncan, Dunraven School, Betty Edwards (Prysor), Betty Edwards (Registrar), Reg Edwards, Gwynfor Evans, Will Evans ('Butch'), Les Hill, Trevor Hitchings (our tea boy!), Tom Hughes, D.J. Hunt, Herbert Hunt, Blodwen Jenkins, Nan Jenkins, Olwen John, Ron John, Roy Jones, John Lawry, John Lazarus, Cynthia Lewis, Cyril Lewis, Bryn Lisle, Trevor Martin, Tony Melville, Ieuan Morgan MBE, Ted Morris, Glenys Owen, Margaret Phillips, Will Scott, Ray Searle, John Smith, Gladys Thomas, Trevor Thomas, Vince Thomas, Treherbert Rugby Club, Treherbert School, Treorchy Rugby Club, Danny Walters, Kay Warren Morgan and Stephanie Thomas of Treorchy Library, Billy Williams, Gary Williams, Vera Williams, Roy Woods.

Our special thanks go to Stephen Winter, for generously loaning us many of his high-quality original postcards for use in the publication; to Treherbert OAP Committee for the use of their hall; and, last but not least, to our wives, Doreen Jenkins and Mavis Green, for their patience and understanding.